GW00457588

THE COMPANY OF HORSES

Peter Fallon

THE COMPANY
OF HORSES

Gallery Books

The Company of Horses
is first published
simultaneously in paperback
and in a clothbound edition
on 13 September 2007.

The Gallery Press
Loughcrew
Oldcastle
County Meath
Ireland

www.gallerypress.com

*All rights reserved. For permission
to reprint or broadcast these poems,
write to The Gallery Press.*

© Peter Fallon 2007

ISBN 978 1 85235 423 7 *paperback*
        978 1 85235 424 4 *clothbound*

A CIP catalogue record for this book
is available from the British Library.

Contents

for Wendell Berry

Go

Then go beyond the reach
of road, lane,
beaten path, or set
of single prints,
deep into the realm
of stillness.

There you bear
the sores and sorrows
of a neighbour,
the illness
of a friend.
There a rock-

pool convalesces
at once after
a spill of rain.
Look out
where landfall
coalesces

with the sea's
sheet iron
and see yourself
for that split
second before
the wind's blade

shreds
the mirror of the bay.
Nothing has stalled
that sound
the length of time.
On any day,

in any weather,
those shards and shatters
glisten.
The morning is telling
you
your life. Listen.

Morning Glory

As if she's
testing the waters
of the stubble,

this hen pheasant
goes to no end
of trouble;

dew, or last night's rain,
still on the stubs of stalks
daubs her brindle bodice

as she bows
with each considered step
before the corn goddess.

Opera

Days

when loose change
feels like money to burn
and the tractor
'takes'
on the second turn

despite a hard frost
and the way it lay
idle a month.
Buds in the hedgerow
are shouting hurray.

You're sawing in sun
and late Easter snows
a windfall,
and the faint blizzard
blows

lightsome delight
across the whole area.
The angel of each blade
of grass is whispering 'Grow'.
Birdsong is an aria

in the opera of desire.
And she says, 'What hurry's
on you? Last to leaf
is longest to linger . . .'
Outside, among snow flurries,

the swallows,
fully fledged and free
as they can be
within the swoops and arcs
of a renewed rhapsody,

lift an already elevated heart
and launch themselves on ways
into the world as if to say,
'Didn't you know, don't forget,
today's

another of those pet days.'

A Holy Show

An early bird. Fighting
cock. Cock of the walk.
His strut. His stop.
His stare declares

he'd tread the whole day
and all the week to come.
He yells at darkness,
'Go to hell' —

a blaze of glory
howling like a heretic
in the bonfire of his infidel
and ruffled feathers.

Fair Game

As if he'd hit
a wall in air,
or slipped on ice,

or simply tripped mid-
flight,
a pheasant stumbles —

then we hear the shot.
All this beside
that stretch of land

in which a farmhand's
fencing.
We see before we hear

the thud.
He's straining wire
as if he's tuning strings

of a long guitar.
And then we come
across the body — a fluster

in the mud,
a final flare
before the fire falters.

The Company of Horses

They are flesh on the bones
of the wind, going full gallop,
the loan of freedom.
But the company of broken

horses is a quiet blessing.
Just to walk in the paddock;
to stand by their stall.
Left to their own devices

they graze or doze, hock to fetlock
crooked at ease, or — head to tail —
nibble withers, hips and flanks.
They fit themselves flat

to the ground. They roll.
But the mere sound or smell
of us — and they're all neighs
and nickerings, their snorts

the splinters of the waves.
And growing out of morning
mists the ghosts of night
form silhouettes along the ridge,

a dun, two chestnuts,
and a bay. A shy colt stares
and shivers — a trembling like
fine feathers in a sudden breeze

around the hooves of heavy
horses. And the dam,
with foal to foot, steadies herself
to find her bearings,

her ears antennae of attention.
Put your hand towards her head-
collar, whispering your *Ohs* and *Whoa*,
Oh the boy and *Oh the girl*,

close your eyes and lean
your head towards
her quiet head, the way
the old grey mare,

hearing that her hero
joined the sleep
of death, spread her mane
across his breast and began to wail and weep.

A Want

As rain's a foe
until there's none
in field or fold
the one

that's missing
is the one
that matters.

Her 'Bring in the sticks.'
'Now?'
Or 'Drive them heifers
from the haggard.'
'Now?'
Her 'Well, are you *nearly*
ready?'
'Nearly.'
Her grumbled 'Nearly
never bulled a cow.'

Once she woke me
with a start.
Cold hands,
cold heart.

Her giving out to the world . . .

And still I'm haunted
by the music of her
'Now where's he gone?
Oh where, oh where?'
And her 'Tell him . . .
Tell him he's wanted.'

The Second Sorrow

And then, when Orpheus
sat lonesome on the sward
and sang his second sorrow
as he played
his stringed instrument,
they came to comfort him
and wrap his tears
in green shade,

the great assembly
of the trees — beeches,
box, limes and laurels,
the motley splash of maples,
parades of cheering palms,
a poplar guard of honour,
the water-loving lotus,
willows too, those staples

of the river bank, all congregated
to console him, ash for shafts
and mountain ash, elms
lending their support to vines,
hazels, firs, the oaks
of Jupiter and holm oaks,
cypress, sycamore,
the trembling tamarisk, and pines —

all snuggled in, beguiled by his lament . . .
And that was long before the time
they scattered on the ground
seeds shaken from a sheaf,
and seeds of poppies, for when
they'd gather in the guise
of birds, the ghosts of those
who'd died of grief.

A Flowering

They were not on the maps.
Notes of their known habitats
recorded nothing
here or hereabouts.

I knew them shy, prized,
arboreal,
from the realm of heraldry.
Were they real at all,

I wondered, till I stood,
a spellbound witness,
downwind of a pair of them.
To have watched them is a richness

I've hoarded
of all my days and doings
as they tied and tied again
the tangles of their to-ings

and fro-ings in the range
of a fallen fir-tree's roots
and I read their conjured script
in the hint of dark July recruits.

And once I touched one.
Car-struck in a storm,
its body warm, its nose-tip cool
as a single boss in a swarm

of blackberries. Years afterwards
I stepped one's trail
in the small relief
of frost which had to fail

in the morning shadows
of the grazing's edge
where it survived, alone
in the margins, fast in a pledge

to thrive and glow
when it emerged, a denizen
of dusk, from nest or mossy hollow,
to flower, now and then again,

in light.

The Blaskets

A word for every wave
that ebbs and flows,
and wind that blows.

Every day's *memento
mori.*
Everybody has a story.

The Orkneys

Be all that as it may,
on a fertile isle
north of here — called Ronaldsay —
short-tailed sheep, their fleeces
shades of red, tan and grey,

have matched their need
between the tides
to newfound feed.
They've salvaged from the rocky shore
a fill of seaweed.

Foragers, ever since the crofters mured
them outside the fields
they conserved for crops. Inured
to it — 'One hand washes
the other' — they've endured.

They've been learning not to care
for ages now,
on scanty fare.
They must slake their thirsts on dew
and other alms of the air.

A Refrain

Their name's a loveliness,
a darling
word, though each of them's
a splashy shitter, marling

the ground beneath their sudden roost,
each of them's one of a flock you'd count
that used to be uncountable, that dimmed
the sun, and now you watch mount

a sycamore and make of it
a vocal chord
until they wheel away, affrighted
or simply of their own accord,

a whim, a whoosh,
a whir.
The rowing wings of, say, a crow
stay solid. Theirs blur.

Then silence. Their one part
chatter, two parts cackle,
betray the part they're mynah
bird or, if you like, southern grackle

working their way, wings
and grey mantle a fletch
of petrol stains,
till some of them fetch

up in the poisoned lands
of new estates, old farms,
their pesticides, while others stall
among the smoke alarms

of the oil fields on fire
along their flight
paths, through the flashpoints of the Tigris
and Euphrates, noon skies as black as night.

Iridescent scavengers,
they'd come and go
across your life,
like that apostle's shadow

healing all it brushed against.
They came and went for years,
a clockwork swipe across September,
and now one reappears,

part of a warbling quarrel,
we say 'Where have you been, starling?
What tales you'd have!'
Our pleas and prayers for you are, *Sing*.

Crane

We watch him
watching us.
Then he picks his way

in slow-
motion through
the minefield of the shore.

Now he unfolds
the parcel of himself
and starts to gather up

the vast contraption of his wings
and crank himself
aloft.

Press ups
and downward pressing
on the bed of air

transform his slack
machinery, grey matter
to a miracle of flight:

hunched heap,
long loper,
sack of shite.

Little Tern, Sea Swallow

A single leaf
of sunlit ivy
that stole onto
a callow tree

reveals a whole
geography —
above, a ridge,
below, a valley,

streams and rivers
worthy
of attention,
seen as you'd see

the x-ray
ecstasy
of little terns in flight,
their tracery

of bones
pure filigree
as they ply their way
across the sky in glory, glory.

Ballynahinch Postcards

AZALEAS: HILARY'S HOUSE

They are the pale
refugees
of Spring —
these buds that push
against the window
opening

on a sheltered nook.
Beyond, midwinter duskus
is a glowering.
But they, they cuddle to
the pane and reimburse its warmth
by January flowering.

≈

CHATELAINE

A winter night
as bright as midnight
in mid-June

a passing cloud
bestows
the curtsy of the moon.

≈

A new-born foal
finding its feet
in the infield;

dun ponies
paddling
in the shallows

of the longer grasses.

≈

A VISITING

I'd been keeping my eyes on
the reeds and rushes,
the bens straddling the horizon,

when I won
my reward — in just one day a hare
and hawk, a waterhen and heron.

≈

They weigh
on you, the sins
of the world,
on such a day

you couldn't
rightly say
where mist ends
and cloud begins.

≈

A day so still
the stones belie
their history —

by the gable of a long
abandoned cottage
a crippled tree

whose apples grew
on a branch
in Eden.

❧

The sudden shock
of meeting them,
dressed to kill.

Then the muffled cries
across a hill
of beaters flushing woodcock,

staccato farts of fowlers' guns.

❧

Rumpled lake,
river rush —
let all our tears

be washed away
like riffles at
forgiving weirs.

❧

I had waited an age
to see this winter bush
again, all life
but little foliage,

a paradigm
of active peace,
where nothing happens
all the time.

❧

Is it any wonder
the tip of Ben Lettery
gleams and glows,

what with the glitter
of a lake lapping
and tickling its toes?

❧

They have turned
their backs to the wind,
trees in that stand,
and yearn for where
the winds don't blow;

they're inclined to the East —
with their prayer mats
of fallen leaves
and all those leaves
strained to know.

❧

I'd begun to think
the like of this
might never strike
again,
the dance of days
in their rightful place.

And when we wanted
music,
there it was —
the rain.

≈

SQUALL

A flock of seabirds
blown to bits —

confetti where
waves wed the shore.

≈

ONE WORLD

Nearly two days after
the tsunami

an extra ripple where
the river bumps into the sea.

≈

'Cheerleaders by the Road
to Clifden, with Pompoms' —
clumps of winter reeds
and grasses

rehearse their flustered repertoire
of Mexican waves
as a fleet of supertankers
passes.

THE MORNING NEWS

You wake up wondering
if Mikey's heifer
calved last night,
a full week beyond her time.

ISADORA

The tide
breathes in, breathes out,
breathes in again.

The beach is basking
in the sea's attention.

She said,
I learned to dance
by watching waves.

STORM

A storm
is happening to the shore. Growls
in the stomach of the surge.
Slaps and smashes. A mastiff's howls.

You,
who'd beware a quiet bull
yet needed to test everything,
could not resist the ocean's pull.

Morning, and the winds
abate.
You leave the mad hounds of the gale
tethered to the garden gate.

GREY

World of wonders.
The slightest shift
of season —
cloud, sunshine,
sun showers, a breeze on

a clear day . . .
                    And she'd
to ask, Why live?
Would she had seen
each of these
could be a reason.

THE SHOW

The tide drags itself ashore
like a slow snore
or the steady action
of a cross-cut saw.

A petrel walks upon the water,
a flash of faith through a gauze
of spray. Breakers crash 'encore'
and ripple their applause.

The broken billows lick their wounds
along the strand: loose threads of brine
unwound and woven back into
the combers that uncurl like a chorus line.

ROCKFALL

Some breakers spend
themselves
and slump towards rockfall.

Some bang
their heads
against the wall

of the headland's end.
The squeal and squall
of a single seabird

you can't see, the all
of it the part of us
calling to be heard.

A Brighter Blue (Ballynahinch Postscript)

At home they've rowed the barley straw
they'll aim to bale today;
so long now since
green May.

For darkening days
are here again,
more than mist,
not quite rain.

And there's a spell
I'd wanted to persist —
though times push past
as the minutes, days and weeks insist.

But who lives in the real
world? So quicken it anew.
Return, replace, repair,
reconstitute, renew.

Turn up the sun!
And put the leaves back
on the trees.
Let river reins hang slack.

Wash the sky
a brighter blue.
Give back to swans
their downy retinue.

Add notes
to summer birds' refrain.
Re-ignite the embers
of rhododendron, Golden Rain.

Resurrect, resuscitate.
Refresh and renovate.
Retrieve, regain and re-install,
translate

everything again. Restore
light moments to the day —
nothing can steal
this while away.

Proprietary

Who owns, he wonders,
as he passes,
these holdings, sites
and old demesnes?

And hears the verdict
of the wind —
trees and brambles,
weeds and grasses.

Pennies and Pounds

He was spreading seed
on a tear in the field,
reprising an ancient refrain
at the thought of the yield:

One for the pigeon,
one for the crow,
one to rot
and one to grow.

His father's fathers
broadcast acres of grain
that was stitched to the ground
by the needles of rain.

Goods hays and harvests —
but their true beatitudes were trees,
hope of the ages,
the crop of histories,

as they heard the holy orders
and mastered persistence,
holding their own
like that oak in the distance.

Like a word to the wise
their revenant chant:
a hundred times more
for the planting than plant.

A Sacrilege

In Ceres' sacred grove there was an oak,
a forest in itself, hung with wreaths
and garlands, kept promises for answered prayers.

No doubt there'd be a price to pay
by him who chose to scorn the gods,
who made no offerings of incense at the altars,
ignored admonishments
and violated ancient woodlands with his axe.

How it shuddered, trembled, groaned
and moaned. How its leaves and acorns
turned an ashen hue.
From the first wound that he inflicted
spurted blood, the way it spills from sacrificial bulls.

❖

And then, out of the heartwood of that tree,
a voice!
        'I who dwell within these branches,
a nymph whom Ceres loves,
damn you with my dying breath.
There is a punishment at hand.
That sureness is my final consolation.'

❖

Ceres then devised a penance
that would have earned its victim
pity had he not forfeited
all claims to sympathy —
the torment of enduring appetite.

You see, there is, far off, a land
whose fields are icefields,
whose earth knows nothing about
crops and trees, and there the corn goddess
enlisted Famine's help and had her wrap
her skinny arms around him — one foul embrace —
and breathe into the hollow veins of Erisychthon.

Then, as seas receive the flows of rivers
and are not overfilled, and fires
any heap of fuel and are not satisfied,
he gorged and gorged
and never knew enough.

His words gave way to groans
and moans and still, enough
was not enough, till he began to bite
and gnaw on his own bones
and ate his heart out and himself away.

(after Ovid)

A Planting

Come June, July,
coltsfoot, fescue and rye outgrew
my seed-started
shoots of yew.

Birch saplings
lorded over beech.
Patience will grant
their proper reach.

Who said we live our lives
elsewhere? Ripeness *is* all.
Barring abuse,
the fruit won't fall

until its time.
And though I rue
the never knowing these
apple trees in their prime, let them do.

Silver Fir

It towers over every
where and thing, that tree
you'd walk
a mile to see

and see from several miles
away. Owl wings
say hush to evening light's
witherings.

First the little, then
the less. Still here
you'll find the woman
of the fields appear,

here, a somewhere
to begin
again, somewhere
to let light in

again — the light,
a glint of light
refracted in the evergreens,
repose of night.

November Rain

The fields are full;
the water tables spilling
through springs and shores.
Rain — and more
to come — overfilling

drains and gullies.
The river's rise,
now that the day's come into light
and the landscape's lake,
slaps patches on the eyes

of the nine-eyed bridge.
'What's happened to my land,
or what you could say *was* my land?'
he wonders as he stares
at his milk-herd on an island . . .

If the known world didn't
the one submerged before us
shrank before our watch,
below low cloud, and the mares
hunched in their uneasy chorus

a warning by the shelter of a wall,
their tails to the wind. What hides
sulking in the plowlands
is water on a giant beach
when the giant tide's

receded. What good could come
of such a deluge, bar it unite us?
Let mud be sap
beneath the bark of winter
to spare the waste of plantings. Heraclitus

only knows where the night
will find us, at home in a dream
of the rest of the country,
hayricks and hedges coming
into their own, and us borne on a stream

to a morning that's exhausted —
a feature in the future almanacs —
the embers of dawn fit to be blazed,
a drying sun ready to rise,
and the breeze blowing lightly, at our backs.

Airs and Angels

They have cast their coats —
oaks and alders,
a bigger beech, cherry trees —
and huddle by the evergreens,
a-shiver in
December's breeze,

fledged with lichen
so profuse you think
they'll suddenly sprout wings,
take flight,
and soar on groundswells
of their own murmurings.

And just as unexpectedly
a stillness turns into a fluttering.
And then the woodland's border flares,
and they take off,
a sparrow troop, put on a show,
become a presence that's all airs

and angels.

A Winter Solstice

A low sun leans across
the fields of County Meath
like thirty watts behind
a dirty blind. New year begins to breathe
new life into the ground.
The winter wheat begins to teethe.

The tarmac streams like precious ore
beside wrapped bales bright in the glare.
Crows shake like collies by a puddle
blooms of spray, and they declare —
a boy's voice breaking in the throat
of morning — a prayer

that works to scour the slate
of unimaginable
hurt. We draw breath in the air —
its shapes are almost tangible —
and the breath and sweat of horses
makes a minor mist — beautiful.

And beautiful the light on water
as the age's newly minted coin.
You'd be hard pressed from here
to tell a withered elm across the Boyne
from an ash that's hibernating.
Past and present join

in the winter solstice.
The days will stretch and we survive
with losses, yes, and lessons too,
to reap the honey of the hive
of history. The yield of what is given
insists a choice — to live; to thrive.

End

i.m. Michael Hartnett (1941-1999)

End of sureness,
end of doubt —

when the darkness
like a light
went out.

Another Anniversary

You turn
hearing the joy
of football
in the yard.
You yearn
for that footfall
of the lost,
the scarred.

Again, again
and again
you feel the sten-
gun attack
of that 'What if?'
and that 'What then?'
Well, then
he'd be a boy

who's ten.

(2000)

Depending on Water

There, just there
where the river bends,
a string that isn't there
suspends

a shoal of shad.
Our light craft lends
itself to water and bears
us as the world intends —

that is, deliberately.
A holiness attends
the times we fished together,
our eyes fixed on the dividends

of confluence, like the hawk
which condescends
to join us, a hawk
and then an osprey, reverends

of an open church,
here, where a river wends
propitiously — the Deerfield river —
or there, among breeze-blown trends

of a little lake in Ireland . . .
We've measured what portends
and worked to make a life
with little call for amends.

For all their loss there's
something in the years that mends.
We've thought and talked about
the need for what transcends

belovèd places
much as their grace commends
them to us — for nothing ends
with family, and friends.

A Will

On a rock, raw rock
knuckling from the ripple
of Lough Ramor,

sprouted from a seed
that was wave-borne
or carried on the claws

of a bird, or spilled
from pockets of the wind,
a sapling —

wind- or wave-worn
but in leaf,
a sprig grappling

to sustain itself
on what?,
a wild oat foraging

in the pasturage
of water,
and holding ground.

Like the split posts
of a locust fence
driven home in earth

to serve one purpose
where they found
another will —

took root
and branched
and blossomed.

Now the living outnumber the dead
and what the dead know
decreases

I learn the lessons of a lake
that says
its story in spray,

or a tree in leaves;
and I say
to my son, my future,

Forgive me,
forgive my frailties and my failings.
I would have my loves outlive me.

The Less Ado

Even as a butterfly's
spread wings, a lake so still,
so clear the image
of the hill

beyond,
you strained to trace
the seam of which is which,
their meeting place,

so the ripple
when it happened
(and it always had to happen)
was a breath of wind

made visible.
Now time's what you've
less of and a friend's
in hospital you move

closer to the gospel
that night
might be best time
to contemplate the light.

You count your blessings.
The evening beats its low tattoo.
You hold your breath. You breathe
again. Every year has two

beginnings.

A Graft

Desired both by gods and demigods,
a host of divine spirits
and the zealous men
who came to her, a thousand supplicants,

her whole world was fruit and herbs,
orchards and fruit fields,
that one nymph whose care was not
for planted woods or wild woodland,

she whose name derived
from what she tended — so she disdained
those who gathered at her gate,
ensconced as she was behind fences,

and slighted that one too
who fed his eye
on her and who fetched up,
first in a harvester's or herdsman's guise,

with ears of corn in wickerwork,
or a goad for oxen, then as a farmhand
or a fisherman, a haymaker
with ropes of hay and wisps of grasses everywhere,

then as a soldier with a soldier's sword,
a vinedresser with secateurs
to tend the tender shoots,
and — once, just once — carrying a ladder

as if he'd pick her garden's fruits;
but she, whose waking thoughts
were of her craft, whole days of prune,
train and graft, turned her back on them

and spurned those suitors, one and all,
until the morning he appeared
in the habit of a hag
whose several kisses were to her

a surprise and a secret prize —
and, as the crone, he spoke of
and for himself:
you were my first love

and will be my last;
if I should die, add to my fame
the years I lost in loving you;
see, he said (still in the rags

of that old woman and her voice),
see yonder elm and how the vine dithers
on it like a dodder and yet thrives —
a thing of beauty, a swarm

of grape clusters and not only
a frame for leaves; see how, alone,
the same vine withers on the ground,
a broken string of beads, a thing of nothing.

Soften your hard heart — and open it —
offer to this hopeless love
a shred of hope so frosts, come late,
won't blight your buds or blossoms,

nor tempests, hail or heavy showers
hijack your fruits and flowers.
And while she pondered this,
he, a shapeshifter, resumed

his proper self and stood before her,
a comely youth whose beauty moved
and won her just as much as his
'I am, and will be, true.

It's not the fruits or herbs
I yearn for most — but *you*.' And then they did
as lovers do, and what occurs to lovers
occurred to them, there in that garden,

the garden of two gardeners.

(after Ovid)

Concerto

From the morning wood
a single bird's
calling card
comes and goes,

comes and goes.
Herald of spring —
though now his earmark's
only echoes.

≋

A hen thrush
on the lawn
upholstered
like an ancient aunt —

and just as curious
when she imagines
you're away, and as affronted
when she finds you aren't.

≋

A wish
like spoken Irish —

the corncrake's rasp
a gasp

for breath.

≋

Who knows,
or who would say,
what goes

unpunished
underneath
the judiciary of crows?

A ratchet turn.
Quickened breath of wings
spins your gaze
westward —

and they grow on you,
those coaly spots,
a crowd of crows rowing
nestward.

The Smithereens

Sun sulking
in a bitter
overcoat. December's runt
of daylight's litter.

Like seconds of a crooked clock
the smithereens
of time drip from the tips
of evergreens,

signs and signals
to embrace.
What lights the moments
only grace?

Are these, you wonder,
proof of God?
And all around you wild things
nod.

It's true, they say, there is
another life but it's within
this one. If they were
opposites who could determine

the one that is
more real?
Or how we'll last? Like trees
that cast their own memorial.

Day and Night

Day — the great adventure
still in store. Time
and time again, one foot
before the other, I climb

among the foothills
that become a life.
We've children now
and I, like my good wife,

must learn the art
of letting go.
For, as Leonardo knew, only
the sun has never seen a shadow.

Night — and the stars shine on
for all they're worth.
I have loved my term
on earth.

Acknowledgements

Grateful acknowledgement is due to the editors and publishers of the following, in which some of these poems were published first: *100 Island Poems* (Iron Press), *Coastline Narratives: Donald Teskey* (Art First, London), *The Clifden Anthology, The Dublin Review, Forgotten Light* (A & A Farmar), *The Irish Reader: Essays for John Devitt* (Otior Press); *Irish Stories of Loss and Hope* (Irish Hospice Foundation), *The Irish Times, Journal of Irish Studies (Tokyo), The Meath Chronicle, Metre, Poetry International, Poetry Ireland Review, An Sionnach, Sunday Miscellany* (RTE Radio) and *TriQuarterly.*

'A Will' was published as a broadside by The Deerfield Press, Massachusetts; 'Depending on Water' by the Robert W Woodruff Library of Emory University. 'A Flowering' was published by The Warwick Press, Easthampton, Massachusetts. Other selections have appeared in limited editions from The Warwick Press (*Morning Glory*, 2006), Press on Scroll Road, Carrollton, Ohio (*Airs and Angels*, with a Foreword by Wendell Berry, 2007) and Ballynahinch Castle, Connemara, in association with Occasional Press, (*Ballynahinch Postcards*, 2007). Special thanks are due to Carol J Blinn, Bob Baris and Des Lally, and — for the door he keeps open at Ballynahinch — Ed Downe.